Are you a Pushy Parent?

How to help your son in the world of soccer

Paúl Fraga

To my father

To Emilie

To my mother wherever she is

CONTENTS

1. <u>DAD, I WANT TO PLAY SOCCER</u>

To begin I'll tell you a story. I don't remember exactly how old I was, about eight or nine. I don't know. The point is that it was a cold Saturday morning and I was going to play the first official game with my classmates. And it wasn't just a simple match, it was a tournament! Imagine how excited we could be.

The night before the match I didn't sleep. That seemed to be Christmas Eve. That morning I could hardly get some breakfast. I couldn't stop. It was as if I had been given a bicycle! My mother was not sure about what to put in the backpack. As it was the first time, she didn't know if we were going to have a shower there, at home, or directly we wouldn't have a shower. That was her only concern. She was worried about me catching a cold! Well, she was worried about that and also about me not getting hurt, so she put into the bag shin guards that were bigger than me. I wanted to wear them even at home, from the beginning (was more cool) but she didn't leave me.

I got the coat, but only that. From the waist down I was dressed in a very athletic way: with shorts and socks halfway up. I had goosebumps because of the cold I had, but I didn't care. Eventually we arrived at the school where the game was going to be played. What a thrill! The parents who were there looked at each other without knowing what to do. We, on the other hand, concentrated in our things.

1

At that time we were getting only a shirt. The rest had to be brought from home by each one of us. Excluding the shirt, the rest of the kit was very colorful. I remember a fellow, whose name I won't tell you here, who, in my opinion, took her sister's shorts because he spent, without exaggeration, the whole match trying to take his trousers off his ass. Can you see the picture? He kept running while trying to accommodate the pants.

It started well... if we had been a flock of birds. More than soccer players we seemed swallows, all behind a ball with an arrow shape. Our team and the opponent as well. In the divided balls that became rugby instead of soccer. Eight kids (it was five a side soccer) on the ball, and the goalkeepers wanting to go as well. They were true scrums.

Like I was saying everything was fine. We were enjoying as true dwarfs we were. We didn't care. We were having a great time. Until the ball left the sideline. Parents started screaming at my teammate as he was going to catch the ball to put it back into play:

-¡Throw in, throw in from the sideline!, shouted at him

-¡Come on, quick, throw in from the sideline!

My teammate, with the ball in his hands, looked at them impassively. Meanwhile, parents kept yelling:

-Quick, pay attention to the sideline and throw in!

Until, suddenly, my teammate, with the ball in his hands, approached a parent of our team and asked him...:

-But... what is the sideline?

No comments. Ignorance is happiness!

As you may know everything starts with, "Dad, I want to play with the school soccer team." By then you receive the request normally. In fact, it is a good thing. I mean, the kid wants to play sports, and soccer is a sport as valid as any other. So, let's let him play!

"Well, I'll have to discuss it with my wife first", you think. "It is also his son and she has to say something. I think she will be ok with that, and, if not, I'll find the way to convince her. That won't be more difficult than when I had to do so to buy the season ticket for the soccer club of the city. That was tough".

-Listen love, before talking to your mother, tell me, when you usually play the games?, you ask.

-Every weekend, he answers.

-Every weekend?, you reply.

-Yes, he confirms.

-And, at what time are usually the games?

3

-The school older boys told us that at 9am every Saturday morning.

-At 9 o´clock in the morning?, you answer quite shocked.

-Yes. Almost always at 9am. Can I play?

You start sweating. It is time to explain that to my wife, you think. Let's see how we manage that. Soccer all weekends and at 9am. In winter as well. That's not very comforting. My wife will agree with that.

-Listen love, also in winter?

-Yes.

"Well, it seems that skiing is over," you think to yourself. "Weekends with my parents or with my in-laws seem that also come to an end. I'm going to miss Friday drinks with friends. My wife won't like that. We will have to go home after coffee. The next day we have to get up early. Everything must be done for the kid.

-Dear, our love has asked me if he can play soccer.

-OK, fine, she answers.

-I just wanted you to know that the games are on Saturday or Sunday at 9am. And in winter too, you explain her

-¿Are you telling me that the kids are playing at 9am including Winter?, she asks you surprised.

-Yes. That is. And they play every weekend.

A simple wish and the whole weekend routine upside down. The whole family conditioned because of soccer. After that everything else comes. You need to buy the material. Boots, shin guards, socks, pants, shirts, bag... That is it. You are already done. You have everything you need. Now its time to start.

Along with the other parents you approach the school to talk with the leaders of the soccer section. You ask all the necessary questions to receive as answers everything that your children had advanced previously. The worst fears are confirmed.

In that small initial informational meeting there are the coaches, the kids (equipped up to the teeth with shin guards that double the size of their tibia, and restless as if was Christmas) and you the parents watching each other. Nobody says anything because nobody knows anything. You just listen. Just listen and think, "will we really need to get up at seven in the morning to leave the kid duly prepared to play the game at 9am? For God´s sake!

2. **THE GAME STARTS**

November 2nd. Saturday. Six forty five in the morning. The alarm sounds.

-It can´t be true, exclaims your wife.

It's over. You have to prepare breakfast and wake your child up. It´s freezing. It is still dark and the streets aren´t built up yet. They have all met in the pitch where the game is going to be played an hour before the start. That is, at 8am. The pitch is 40 miles away. There is almost no time to have a shower or have breakfast properly.

After breakfast and after dressing the child for the cold, but, you know, with shorts and with your kid proud of his shin guards, you turn to the pitch. The odyssey begins.

When you arrive, the child comes into the circle where his friends are. You, still bleary, have a look to each other as saying to yourself what the hell are we doing here. But something must be done. It's 8am and we have an hour to go yet.

After stretching a little bit you start looking for a place to go. At that time, so early in the morning, only a couple of bars are opened giving breakfast. "A hot coffee would be great", you say to yourself. In order to avoid getting too embarrassed you choose a bar where there is someone already. You want to have coffee as unnoticed as possible.

You, parents, start discussing. The first conversation turns around the early time and how freezing it is. Nobody understands anything. You are there because your children want to play soccer. Nobody knows if they are good, bad or just the opposite. Nobody has the slightest idea. Today will be the first time you see them play.

It's time for the match. You, the parents, split into two groups. On one hand, we have mothers. On the other hand, fathers. Mothers do nothing but complain about how cold it is and the early time. All of them afraid of their children catching a cold or even worse, catching pneumonia. Soccer is not that important. "The important thing is that the kids have fun playing sports," they say.

You, the fathers, are expectant. You don´t talk too much. You still do not have much confidence and also there is some tension there. You are all eager to be proud of your children. But you are not because you have not seen them play yet. And that creates a disturbing anxiety. By now, you have forgotten the cold. Anxiety overcomes. "Son, make me proud of you," many of you think. There are doubts about what you are about to see.

3. **FIRST KICKS TO THE BALL**

A fifteen years old boy "crazy" enough to be the referee so early, gives the opening whistle. The game starts in the pitch ... and out of it.

That is not a soccer game. That's like a flock of birds in migration going behind the ball. Mothers encourage. They are their little children. If you are better or worse is irrelevant. Another thing goes on in the father's bench. You can see the first smiles ... and the first twisted gestures. It all depends on what you see and the player who has done it.

From the first moment you begin to see who has enough conditions, some conditions or, directly, no conditions. Doesn't take much time to realize. A simple ball touch is enough to know if a kid has idea and coordination.

The competition has already started. But it has started off the pitch. In the stands. You are no longer the same parents. Now, you are the parent of the good kid, the parent of the star, the parent of the bad player and the parent of the kid that doesn't play. All parents with your own pride. Mothers keep screaming and cheering. They are more concerned about their children not getting hurt than anything else. Perfectly understandable, by the way.

As parents you have already dispelled your doubts. Everything is clear now. Now everyone takes his own pride out covertly. Never in an evident way. But sideways.

The match has started in the parent's bench. Not even in the pitch. The kids play as if they were in the school playground. In the pitch there are only smiles and joy. Is the parent´s crafty side that begins to emerge.

The kids have only just started playing but that is already enough for you parents to either keep your pride calm or crack it and be ashamed as result. Everything because of what you see and your particular interpretation of those things you see, comparatively speaking. Objectivity ceases and gives way to subjectivity. In fact, objectivity has never existed at this point. Only subjectivity. As we are all subjects. The children, meanwhile, in the pitch, having fun.

The game finishes. Nothing is the same no more. New "mental maps" have been already created. One per each parent. What has been seen matters, but not as much as the interpretation that each parent has done about what he has seen. We have a broth already. Why? Because each parent according to his particular mental map has already decided which are his most absolute truths. Subjective truths which are considered by each of you as objective science. "My son is brilliant. That is it". "If he hasn´t played well is because his teammates don´t pass him the ball, or more directly, the coach does not trust him. He is always picking on him". "Why has the coach replaced my son and not any other kid?" "It's not fair. That kid hasn´t done anything".

It is already known. Give me an interest or a goal and I will give you reasons to justify it. Pride is inversely proportional to criticism. In soccer there are no absolute truths. Everything is debatable. And opinion is a filter. It is like a software that receives an input from the outside which is processed. And it does it depending on how the "mind software" has been set. From there on you get an output that will be expressed, and may or may not coincide with the others beliefs.

This should lead to many discussions. They are disputes that arise because each parent has its own reality, and pretends the rest to have his same vision. And that is not possible. Every parent has his own reality because each one has his own interests according to his goals and passions. Everything begins with a "it´s my little child" and from there on each one creates his own scenario, the software that, thereafter, will process everything that will happen, in general, and will happen to your child, in particular. That has always happened and will always happen.

The children leave the locker room. All of them with a smile. A couple of them maybe grumbling because of the result but usually everyone is happy. Each one looking after his parents and waiting for the first signs of approval, the first words of support, of recognition. That's the first test.

There's the first choice of a parent. On one hand, it's your son and you love him , but the parent has his mind already tainted by comparison. The child hasn´t played alone. He has played with other people. The parent will drop a, "All right son. You've been great. Did you have fun ?" And the child will answer yes while eating a chocolate sandwich and drinking Coca Cola. But the parent has told his son a half-truth. Or a white lie. He has said what his child wants to hear, but the parent knows very well what he has really seen. If your child is not first class, an endless race starts in the parent´s head, which is no other than, permanently, try to adapt the actual facts to his wishes. What causes a permanent status of misinterpretation. A perpetual scene of self-deception. A deception disguised as reality. He will always see the facts under the scrutiny of his software , his own reality . But that reality will be false. It is affected by desire. As parents you have already lost the objectivity and you've gone down to subjectivity. The only thing that happened between one situation and the other is the appearance of the same facts affected by different emotions. As many as parent-child relationships are.

From the "whole picture" of the previous match, parents, mainly the father, begin a process of "fine rain" with his child . That is, the parent will speak to his child releasing a number of issues and ideas concerning him, his teammates, the coach or the team. It's a kind of a gradual mind poisoning although is well intentioned: "Why did the coach put you as a defender? You're striker. You asked him to do so?" "Why were you in the bench as replacement? You are

11

much better than any other of your team". "I saw a teammate of yours that didn´t want to pass you the ball. I think he wants to be the only one to score". And so on and so forth. Although there is no doubt that this is a well-meaning attitude, the truth is that they are continuously introducing in his children mind subjective judgments disguised as absolute truths. Children at that early age consider you as models and accept every assessment you may give. With ten or eleven years old they have no critical thinking and thus they lack of barriers to prevent any form of mental poisoning.

You, parents, unconsciously and with the laudable intention of helping your children, begin to guide their behavior in relation to them and soccer under particular judgments and many parents begin to lose perspective. The most important is that what is really important, matters most. Kids at this age just want to play soccer with his friends. Just that. The rest is not needed.

The second match day arrives. This time at 9:30am, and thirty miles away from home. We are making progress. It is still freezing. As always, jacket, jersey, two shirts and hat. However, shorts with shocks, boots and shin guards. That doesn´t change. But what has changed is the willingness with which parent and son face this second game.

In the first match, you, as a parent, were expectant. You had no reviews to do because you didn´t know what you were about to see. Meanwhile, your child was facing the match with the enthusiasm and anxiety that is characteristic in those who have no idea of what they are about to find, but who are absolutely convinced that they are going to love it.

For this second game something has changed. This time, during the trip, parent and son are no longer in silence. The child, instead of going to the match with a virgin mind, has already a "low cost" version of your mind map. Your reviews have been positioning and he can start creating his own filter to pass the reality through. Thereafter nothing will be exactly the same.

You arrive to the pitch. It is possible that this time your wife and daughter have stayed home. There is no curiosity now. They already know what is going on and they think about pros and cons. The child gets out the car and calls his friends. You parents, meanwhile, begin your pilgrimage to the bar. This time you talk. You do it timidly but you begin to share opinions. "Hey, your son kicks the ball very well, eh. He has quality". "How is your son? Happy?", asks one . "Well, yes, but he is a striker and he is playing as a defender", answers. They are tense calm moments. Personal criteria confirmation moments. Moments where opinions are contrasted. If a parent feels the same as me, he knows about soccer. Just the opposite if he doesn´t. He thinks my son is a good player? If he does, he has criteria, if not... Philias and phobias start being created. The particular "labeling" begins. Remember that each parent assumes his opinion as an absolute truth. But, as everything is debatable, there are different truths.

By the time that coffees are paid, each parent will have already perfectly cataloged each "pack" parent-son. You will have subjectively associated behavior patterns. "The child is very bad and the parent justifies it by saying that he hasn´t played in his place. He has no idea of soccer", or, "your son seems to be a good player but I didn´t like his smile. He is a little bit cocky". And so on so forth.

There is always a parent that due to timidity or prudence always remains quieter. He just listens and draws conclusions. Your child may not be good enough to play soccer. Perhaps, like the rest of his teammates, he wanted to play just to have fun and spend time with his friends. However, a parent doesn´t find nice to realize that his kid doesn´t give the minimum level. Am I ok? It is painful. To overcome that a lot of perspective is needed, as well as a great self-esteem. You have to learn how to take the drama out of it in order to avoid getting involved in useful and painful feelings. It´s not pleasant for anybody to see your loved ones limitations so obviously. And it´s even worse if he is 10 years old. All that makes the parent feel bad, and unfortunately he will end up associating the performance of his child in the pitch with his personal inner discomfort. And that is a dangerous situation.

In such scenario, the parent only has two possibilities. On one hand, there is always the possibility to tell your child the truth. That it would be better to try another sport. But you think: how can you say that to your son? He wants to be with his friends! Enjoy playing sports with them. A parent can´t deny that desire to his child. He plays soccer in a generous way and has fun with it. What more can a parent ask for? Well, maybe for not having to see him and for being able to ignore the opinions from other parents which cause so much pain. Or even more difficult. Becoming immune to everything around him. That requires a hard work training.

On the other hand, being aware that you can´t tell your child that soccer is not his thing, pushes you to think that there is no choice but trying to improve his performance. We have, therefore, the first "pushy parent". Thereafter all opinions will be biased. Everything will be taken to improve the faculties of the kid.

In a process of systematic deception, the parent will complain because the coach can´t take out of his child the faculties that only his parent thinks he has. We began to hear in the games things such as "Son, don´t pay attention to your coach. He doesn´t know. You must play here". "Pass the ball to this or that player". "As soon as you have a chance, shoot". You enter into a self-destructive spiral where the parent projects his frustrations, desires, wishes in the child. With a total absence of self-criticism.

Everyone knows that the blame is always on the other. The kid is good because I say so, and if anyone thinks the opposite is because everyone has been alienated to think so.

The kid, in the pitch, incredulous. He doesn´t understand anything about the things he sees and hears. In fact, he doesn´t know who to ignore. On one hand you have the coach saying one thing and on the other hand his parent nonstop talking saying what he should and shouldn´t do, as well as talking badly about the coach.

It is clear that parent and son are living different realities. There is no coherence between what the child is looking for with sport and what he is perceiving from his parent. The child doesn´t understand his parent´s reactions and his attitude. There is no causal link between what he, as a son, feels and looks for playing soccer with his friends and the attitude that his parent is having. And that is disturbing. The kid doesn´t understand anything. And the substantial difference is that while the behavior of the child is based on having fun, the parent's interest lies in getting rid of his inner discomfort and personal frustrations. The child has a simple positive motivation to do what he does, and the parent has a complex negative motivation.

This situation, which is complicated, has more chapters. There are more games to play and all of them are played at home. At each child home. Each one of them with his parents. All of you have opinions and all of you draw conclusions. The parent of the good guy, will adore his son because of the emotion. He is already projecting a promising future. The son doesn´t care. It's flattering but it´s not that important for him. His has other interests. Possibly his parent, conscious of the good qualities of his child, will talk about the less gifted boy indifferently. The son, who obviously can´t escape from home, will be gradually permeated by his parent´s ideas (light rain). His parent begins to be his opinión generator.

That happens in every house. In yours as well. It also happened in mine. No matter if it is in the good boy or bad boy house. The behavior is the same. The only difference is the message.

Games go by, and what, originally, was a group of children with a virginal mentality ends up, as time passes by, in a group of guys with different realities. With bias. Meanwhile the coach trying to make a team out of that, and bringing interests together. Interests that gradually have been getting more and more dispersed. In fact, the first dissident figures begin already to appear. And we're talking about children. That deserves a critical reflection, don´t you think?

But that is not all. Envies begin to arise. Supporters and detractors. The little groups. All the "if you are not with me, you are against me". The inner pain, which at first was only suffered by the parent after being face to face with the reality that his child wasn´t good enough to play soccer, has been inevitably transmitted to the child. Emotions work as the theory of communicating vessels. Like a seed that is planted in the mind (dads subjective valuation), you water (constant repetition of the same message: light rain) and that ends up growing (the child has eventually created a partial picture depending on what he has heard from his parent who is his main opinion generator).

The truth has not been told to the child (that he is not good enough) to avoid hurting him. Whereupon the father transmits the kid that it is not his fault, that are the circumstances that are not adequate (teammates, coach, wrong positions in the pitch, etc..). It is pretended to hide the reality to the child throwing him the wrong message. Although it is a well-meaning message. This forces the parent to adapt the objective reality to his own reality. A reality that is no other than the one that he is throwing in his message. To achieve this goal, he will spare no effort: running the game from the sideline, discrediting the coach and anyone likely to show his child the true reality. I understand that the ultimate goal is to act as a shield, but the pain is not avoided, it´s only postponed.

As a result the child has a false picture of reality that will generate him a mental map that will get him nowhere, concerning soccer. The child eventually will end up realizing which are his limitations. However, along the way he will already have experienced some frustration episodes.

Einstein used to say that: "If you put a fish climbing a tree, the fish will always think that he is useless." Is the ego, and the intention to adapt reality to your beliefs, what actually makes people "keep climbing and not swimming".

Games continue to be played. Every parent and every child have created their own mental maps based on their priorities. Soccer matches have become two face games. On one hand there are those who do not fulfill the necessary conditions, those you know will not have a future in this sport. On the other hand, are those that could potentially arrive. I will not get into whether or not they will dedicate to this because it depends on many things and, moreover, it is not the goal I have for this book. Maybe in another.

In the first group, parents run the game from the sideline in order to try to adapt realities and also look for excuses and justifications. There are some that scream, that screech and complain loudly. But there are also those that say nothing. That are in silence. Do you recognize yourself in any group? In both situations the inner pain that a parent is experiencing is double . On one hand, because of seeing patently the lack of conditions of his child (although absolutely nothing happens. Soccer is not his thing and that is it . It's nothing serious) . And on the other hand there is envy. Envy because his son is not like the one that stands out. And we already know that ego can´t handle that. Ego acts in two ways. Tries to excel when he is conscious of his ability, and tries to equate when he has not the level.

Therefore, he will try to belittle attitudes that stand out (will try again to adapt reality to his desires) to find a balance where his child can also be compared. It's like being a millionaire. This can be because you earn a lot (excel above) or because you don´t spend (you look for the balance below).

"Men can handle with others being praised as long as they think that actions being praised can be also done by them" Tucidides.

Between these parents there are those who, as already has be explained, remain in silence. The fact that they remain in silence doesn´t mean they don´t act as explained. The only difference is that they don´t express it as a "pushy parent". They just ponder over. Different responses to the same realities. But the feeling of inner dissatisfaction is the same. And the envy that they have can be even worse. **The envious silence is full of noises.**

Those noises that are stated in those who express their feelings.

"Moral indignation is just jealousy with halo". George Herbert

However, those parents with children who hoard conditions are not away from dissatisfaction. So far, this inner discomfort was motivated by personal interpretations or by other parent´s comments. Things change as children get older and go up in different categories. What before were particular interpretations begin to be third party interpretations, from outside the environment of the young player: Club scouts and regional coaches appear.

By that time, those kids who didn´t meet the necessary conditions have already suffered the disappointment of realizing the true reality. **As we get older we are more aware of our limitations. We create our own criterion. And we reach a moment where we seek congruence between what we are and what we have been told we were.** And our look turns normally to our parents.

That's when we start considering many of the things we have heard. In the end, some parents, with the goal of doing no harm, twist his child´s environment to delay the self-esteem damage, and ultimately will be his own children who will realize how things really are. Then disappointment comes. But not everything is bad. You finish to overcome disappointment and, what's even better, when one is aware of his condition ends up enjoying sport greatly, no matter what sport is it, and despite all the limitations. We return to what once was soccer. That first match day. That November 2nd five years ago.

The figure of the "pushy parent" remains. The only thing that change are the interpreters. With the appearance of such third party qualified opinion there is no more a breakdown between good and bad. And if so, does not worry anymore. What starts worrying is the choice between good and better. At this age and in those school teams, what the coach says begins to worry less and more what these figures of qualified opinion think. So history repeats itself. The comments you start hearing around begin to hurt. **There is nothing more painful than comparison**. And if it´s between same level players is even worse. What before were congratulations because you used to win, now are concerns. "What does he think about my son?" "Would he like it?" "Does he want to sign him?" Maybe he prefers this one who is also good and not my son". "That can be true? My son is much better".

As we can see, we go back to the beginning. The context changes but not the content. Basic instincts are concerned and emerge. Up to the point that **the parent´s emotional well-being about soccer and his child performance is closely linked to a third party opinion.** It's not a capacity issue. Now it's a matter of choice. You want to be the elected one, you do not want the other to be elected. That's the goal. And the parent's behavior will be focused towards that. Such behavior creates stress, which is caused by uncertainty. Every person is aware that not everything is under control. And the human being hates uncertainty. Can´t tolerate not knowing what will happen. And if you don´t have emotional self-control critical parents, even with coaches and teammates, begin to appear. It is known that **envy doesn´t smile, envy likes grimacing**.

That unease is also transmitted, and does it basically to the kid. The child is charged with a responsibility that doesn't belong to him.

As in the "good and bad" breakdown, in the "good and better" breakdown all comes down to comparison. The human being can't tolerate comparison. Only does it if he wins. After that everything else comes. Self-deception as well.

"Greatness inspires envy, envy engenders resentment, resentment produces lies". Joanne Kathleen Rowling.

Time heals everything and suddenly what initially produced anxiety and sleeplessness, eventually becomes situation understanding. It is an act of self-accommodation. Man can't be uncomfortable permanently. Instinctively the human body seeks its own welfare, and that comes when we assume the objective reality, not the interested one.

That's why parents end up assuming third party decisions that, through the figure of their children, directly affect them. Now there is no intention to change anything. You just start to take things as they come. It is symptomatic that as things clarify, as things get clear, the sideline activity, the pushy parents activity decreases. The situation gets more normal. There are no expectations to fulfill. Interests no longer appear on the way. The future is now. Nothing surprises. Children have the conditions they have and the decisions of others are already taken. So the only thing to do is enjoy the journey. Quietly. We return to the beginning. Let´s play!

4. ISSUES TO CONSIDER

I know that everything I'm going to say now may seem very difficult to do. Maybe it´s true. In these lines the only thing I want is to indicate a number of issues that I think you might find helpful. According to this, success is closely related to reflection. A priori it is very difficult to control sudden reactions, however it´s interesting that you are aware of what has happened and is happening to you, and stop the pulses that you as a parent can ever have.

First, if you want to help your child in these issues you have to **break any kind of emotional attachment**. Many of the problems between the "pushy parents" and their children is motivated by parents high vulnerability. Emotional attachment produces dependence, and this one produces vulnerability. Some parents idealize the sporting performance of their children and when their expectations aren´t met they feel disenchanted and injured. And that causes to the child a gradual mind poisoning with the only intention of relieving their own pain. Parents are victims of expectation.

Second, you need to have the **context clear and maintain focus**. Don´t forget that all starts because the kid wants to play soccer with his friends. Everything else that is created around is, figuratively, science fiction movies with special effects. They are artificially created realities and feelings. From subjective considerations. Reality is different and responds to other issues. **Don´t forget that**

you suffer more because of what you imagine rather than because of what actually happens.

Third, **distraction control**. It has much to do with the point above. The lack of self-confidence makes us accept others' opinions, third party opinions, as absolute truths, which influence our behavior and our comments with our children.

Fourth, **do not pay attention to those issues that are beyond your control.**

Fifth, **mental strength** to carry all this out. Each one´s soccer conditions can be refined but can´t be created. They are what they are. Accept it. But having good conditions is a necessary thing but is not enough. Many times the main difference is mental strength. The difference is in how we face the challenges without diverting from the chosen path. Without paying attention to anything that doesn´t provide the slightest value.

5. <u>CONCLUSIONS</u>

I don´t know if you, as a reader, have felt yourself identified with all you have just read. If not, congratulations, you´re doing the appropriate. If, on the contrary, you have seen yourself reflected in any passage of the book, stay calm, it´s not that serious. It has solution. Don´t worry.

I wanted to write this because I think it can help to many parents who want to help their children in their emerging soccer career. They have been many years playing and watching soccer. This type of behavior is not something isolated. It is a recurring behavior. It's a *déjà vu*. And I can say that, after being a direct witness you need to have in mind this book. I encourage you to treat your child, according to soccer (or any other sport), in "third person". Literally. That would be better for you but above all much better for your son. Behaving like this takes time. True. Needs training. True. But is the appropriate behavior. Now you just have to put it into practice. Go ahead.

Follow me:

<u>Twitter</u>: @PaulFraga

www.futbolydineroresponsable.com